THE LITTLE JOHN

JOHN I

MAPS AND PHOTOGRAPHS BY
JOHN N. MERRILL

a J.N.M. PUBLICATION

1988

a J.N.M. PUBLICATION

JNM PUBLICATIONS,
WINSTER,
MATLOCK,
DERBYSHIRE.
DE4 2DQ

Conceived, edited, typeset, designed, marketed and distributed by John N. Merrill.

© Text and routes — John N. Merrill 1986 and 1987

© Maps and photographs — John N. Merrill 1987

First Published — October 1986
This edition — February 1988

ISBN 0 907496 46 6

Meticulous research has been undertaken to ensure that this publication is highly accurate at the time of going to press. The publishers, however, cannot be held responsible for alterations, errors or omissions, but they would welcome notification of such for future editions.

Set in Futura: Light, Medium and Bold.

Printed by: Linprint, Mansfield, Nottinghamshire.

CONTENTS

ABOUT JOHN N. MERRILL

John combines the characteristics and strength of a mountain climber with the stamina, and athletic capabilities of a marathon runner. In this respect he is unique and has to his credit a whole string of remarkable long walks. He is without question the world's leading marathon walker.

Over the last ten years he has walked more than 55,000 miles and successfully completed ten walks of at least 1,000 miles or more.

His six walks in Britain are—

Hebridean Journey	1,003 miles
Northern Isles Journey	913 miles
Irish Island Journey	1,578 miles
Parkland Journey	2,043 miles
Lands End to John O'Groats	1,608 miles

and in 1978 he became the first person (permanent Guinness Book Of Records entry) to walk the entire coastline of Britain—6,824 miles in ten months.

In Europe he has walked across Austria (712 miles), hiked the Tour of Mont Blanc and GR20 in Corsica as training! In 1982 he walked across Europe—2,806 miles in 107 days—crossing seven countries, the Swiss and French Alps and the complete Pyrennean chain—the hardest and longest mountain walk in Europe.

In America he used the world's longest footpath—The Appalachian Trail (2,200 miles) as a training walk. The following year he walked from Mexico to Canada in record time—118 days for 2,700 miles.

During the summer of 1984, John set off from Virginia Beach on the Atlantic coast, and walked 4,226 miles without a rest day, across the width of America to San Francisco and the Pacific Ocean. This walk is unquestionably his greatest achievement, being, in modern history, the longest, hardest crossing of the USA in the shortest time—under six months (177 days). The direct distance is 2,800 miles.

Between major walks John is out training in his own area —the Peak District National Park. As well as walking in other areas of Britain and in Europe he has been trekking in the Himalayas four times. He lectures extensively and is author of more than sixty books.

INTRODUCTION

I first began exploring The Dukeries area on foot in the 1960's, when I spent four years wooing a girl from Worksop—to no avail! The legacy of the relationship is my appreciation of the walking potential of the area. It may not be mountainous but it does have very attractive forests, unspoilt villages, meandering rivers, folklore and a place where you are not likely to meet other walkers, even in mid summer. Since 1970 I have wanted to write a walk guide to the area, and this ambition was fulfilled in 1986 when after spending more then six months walking the area, my book 'Short Circular Walks in the Dukeries', was published.

One of my walking book themes has been the creation of a day challenge walk of around 25 miles in length that anyone can do. Using my short walk book as a guide I began piecing together a route linking together my favourite areas. The result is this book! My aim was simple:
   1. a route long enough to challenge the average person when walked in a day
   2. keep to as much forest as possible
   3. being flat country I felt an extra three miles to my usual criterion would stretch the individual and no trail profile would be needed
   4. keep it as remote as possible—apart from two inns and a shop there are no amenities until the final stages.

Bearing in mind these points I gradually walked the route in stages, endeavouring to include as many features of the area as possible to illustrate its well known characteristics. I hadn't planned on passing three sewage works on the route but that was a fact of the final layout. After three months of sorties into the area I was ready to walk it in one go. On July 5th 1986, I made the inaugural walk. All week the weather had been hot and sunny. Typically, on the 5th it was cloudy and cool with a violent rain storm part way round approaching Creswell Crags. Perhaps it was a blessing in disguise and ideal walking conditions. Walking 9 hours without stopping I completed the circuit, having seen only four walkers!

The highlights for me were the attractive village of Cuckney and its church, the stretch of woodland from South Lodge in Welbeck towards Truman's Lodge, Clumber, and the woodland and rivers at Conjure Alders. As usual I drank no liquid all day and only ate three bars of chocolate. Regaining Edwinstowe I felt tired and my legs knew they had been pushed hard, but I felt pride in completing such an attractive forest walk. I can only hope you too have such an enjoyable walk exploring the area and seeing for yourself its many sided facets. Have a good walk and may the sun shine and the wind be always at your back; let me know how you fared.

Happy Walking,   *John N. Merrill*

JOHN N. MERRILL
Derbyshire 1986

HOW TO DO IT

The whole route is covered by the Ordnance Survey map—1:50,000 series—Sheet No 120—Mansfield, Worksop & surrounding area. This map is ideal for basic planning and support party use, but for actual walking of the route the following four Ordnance Survey maps, 1:25,000 Pathfinder series, will be found extremely useful.

> Sheet SK66/76—Ollerton
> Sheet SK46/56—Mansfield (North) & part of Sherwood Forest
> Sheet SK47/57—Worksop (South) & Stavely
> Sheet SK67/77—Clumber Park and East Markham

The whole walk is devised to be completed in a single day, allowing 9 to 12 hours. There is no criterion to walk it in a day—it is not a competition—and if you want to spend a weekend over it, that's fine. There are few facilities actually on the route and you are best to be fully prepared for all eventualities and be self contained—see amenities guide. For those who complete the walk a special four colour embroidered badge and completion certificate is available from JNM Publications. A master record of all who walk the route is maintained by them.

Jousting in Sherwood Forest

EDWINSTOWE AND SHERWOOD FOREST—according to legend, Edwin, King of Northumberland, who died at the Battle of Hatfield in 632 was buried in the woods near the present village site. The word Stowe means the holy or burial place. St. Mary's Church is said to be the place where Robin Hood and Maid Marion were betrothed. The nearby Visitor's Centre has an exhibition to Robin Hood and his merry men. Paths lead to Major Oak, the largest oak tree in England and the hideout for Robin Hood and his men. The forest was once quite extensive and the area close to Edwinstowe, known as Birklands and Bilhaugh, were surveyed in 1658. In 840 acres there were 11,000 oak trees and 5,000 other trees.

ROBIN HOOD AND LITTLE JOHN—one of the great folk-heroes of England, but very little true evidence to ascertain whether he and his men existed. Nottinghamshire and Derbyshire are littered with place-names to the two heroes and Little John is buried in Hathersage churchyard in the Derbyshire Peak District. Little John was Robin Hood's second in command.

WELBECK ABBEY—is private but can be glimpsed as you walk round before and after Creswell Crags. The buildings are now used by Welbeck College but are the work of the Dukes of Portland. Everything is on a grand scale; the Riding School, for instance, measures 385 feet long by 112 feet wide. Holbeck church has many memorials to the Portland family.

CLUMBER PARK—the 3,800 acre park was originally the home of the Duke of Newcastle. The fifth Duke in the mid 18th century planted the double lime tree avenue—Duke's Drive—and at a mile long is the longest double lime avenue in Europe. 100 years ago the house was extensive but a major fire in 1897 destroyed many of the rooms. In 1938 the house contents were sold and the estate became part of the National Trust. Hardwick Village was largely built by the Newcastles for their estate workers.

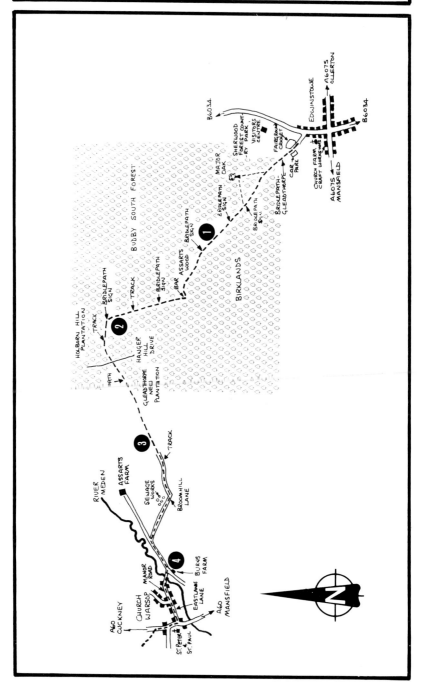

EDWINSTOWE TO CHURCH WARSOP—
4½ MILES

ABOUT THE SECTION—

The first three miles are all in forest, with the option of making a detour to see the renowned Major Oak. It is all along well defined tracks/paths but, as there are several paths in some areas, attention to your route line is advised. You emerge from Gleadthorpe New Plantation into fields and continue on a good path towards Church Warsop.

MAPS—*1:25,000 O.S. Pathfinder Series—Sheet SK 66/76—Ollerton 1:25,000 O.S. Pathfinder Series—Sheet SK 46/56—Mansfield (North) and part of Sherwood Forest.*

WALKING INSTRUCTIONS—

From the car park near the fairgrounds and cricket ground, turn right along the path through the grounds past the bridlepath sign— Gleadthorpe and Major Oak. Shortly afterwards enter the forest. ¼ mile later reach a crossroads of paths and keep straight ahead; the one to your half right leads to Major Oak. By turning left at the tree you will return back to the route. Another ¼ mile brings you to another path junction—this is where the Major Oak path joins. Again basically keep straight ahead, guided by metal bridlepath signs. You pass another in about three minutes and in another ¼ mile another beside path crossroads. Here bear half left on the wide path as you begin bearing left through Assarts Wood. A little over ¼ mile you gain a track with a bar across your path, and bridlepath sign opposite. Turn right along the track, and the main path-following problems are behind you. Keep on the track for the next ½ mile.

Again as guided by the bridlepath sign, turn left onto another track with metal bar across and continue through more plantation. A little over ¼ mile you gain the tarmaced surface of Hanger Hill Drive. Go straight across onto another track and a few yards later this turns left. Keep ahead on the path which keeps close to the edge of Gleadthorpe New Plantation. After nearly ½ mile you emerge into fields. Keep on the path beside the field boundary on your right. At the end of the second field you enter the track of Broomhill Lane which you follow around the sewage works; now becoming a tarmaced surface. At the T junction beyond turn left, and opposite Burns Farm, right over the River Meden and into Manor Road. At the road junction keep ahead along Eastlands Lane to the A60 road in Church Warsop, with the church to your right.

CHURCH WARSOP TO CUCKNEY—2 MILES

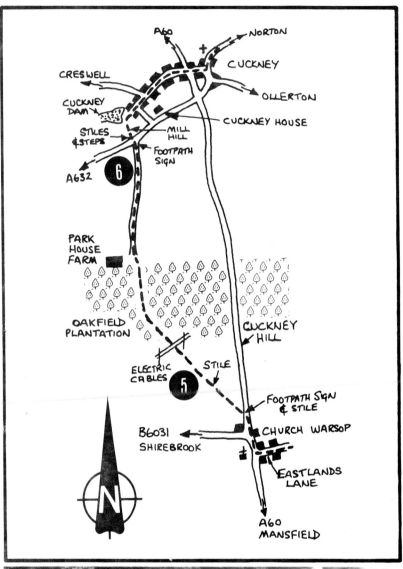

Cuckney Dam

6

CHURCH WARSOP TO CUCKNEY—2 MILES

ABOUT THE SECTION—

A short gentle climb on a faint path brings you back briefly into forest before descending towards Cuckney. The village is entered via its dam and is full of historical interest and contains the first inn on the walk.

MAPS—*1:25,000 O.S. Pathfinder Series—Sheet SK 46/56—Mansfield (North) and part of Sherwood Forest. 1:25,000 O.S. Pathfinder Series—*
Sheet SK 47/57—Worksop (South) & Staveley.

WALKING INSTRUCTIONS—

Walk past the church on your left and keep on the A60 road for 100 yards to the stile and footpath sign on your left. The path is little used but you ascend half to your left to the top lefthand corner of the field, where there is a stile. Continue ahead to the top lefthand corner of the next field where there is a gap. You are heading for the lefthand edge of Oakfield Plantation, gained after passing under the electric pylons. In the forest corner bear right onto a track and turn immediately left onto a path which keeps just inside the lefthand edge of the plantation. After ¼ mile reach the main forest, turning right then left onto a track, and continue descending through the forest and passing Park House Farm, a field away to your left.

At the end of the forest turn left then right onto the tarmaced farm drive and follow this due north to the A632 road ½ mile away. Cross the road and ascend the steps and two stiles and follow the path around Mill Hill and descend to Cuckney Dam. Turn right along School Lane, bearing right at the end along Creswell Road into Cuckney. Cross the A60 into Budby Road to the Greendale Oak Inn and turn left down Norton Lane.

CUCKNEY—the 18th century mill, dam and buildings remain unspoiled in this picturesque village. The church dedicated to St. Mary, is surrounded by an earthwork. The church dates from Norman times and is built upon a mass grave, where about 200 people were buried; the cause of their demise is unknown. The Greendale Oak Inn records a famous tree in Welbeck estate. The Duke of Portland wagered he could drive a coach and four through the tree which had a 40 foot circumference. A 10 foot high by 6 foot wide hole was cut through the tree and the Duke rode through! Cuckney is named after Thomas de Cuckney who in the 12th century founded the Welbeck estate.

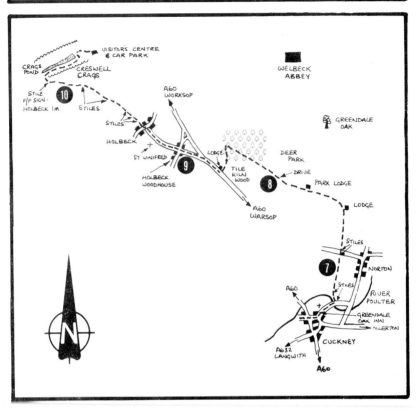

Creswell Crags

CUCKNEY TO CRESWELL CRAGS—4 MILES

ABOUT THE SECTION—

A mile of walking across the fields brings you into Welbeck Park where you walk along the driveway through woodland, catching glimpses of the Abbey and deer. You continue the Welbeck theme towards Holbeck, passing the church where several of the Portland family are buried. Beyond are further fields before entering the limestone gorge of Creswell Crags.

MAP—*1:25,000 O.S. Pathfinder Series—*
Sheet No SK 47/57—Worksop (South) & Staveley.

WALKING INSTRUCTIONS—

Leave Cuckney via Norton Lane passing the Church St.Mary on your left. Cross the River Poulter and turn left at the stile and path sign. The path ascends to the trees on the small escarpment to a wooden stile. The other side you gain fields and keep the field boundary on your immediate right for just over ¼ mile to the minor road to Norton. Cross over to the next stile and path sign, now keeping the field boundary on your immediate left. At the end of the second field pass through a kissing gate and gain the driveway of Welbeck, opposite a lodge and impressive gateway. Turn left, and as guided by the footpath sign follow the tarmaced driveway. You keep on it for the next 1¼ miles. En route passing Park Lodge on your right and ½ mile later entering Tile Kiln Wood.

¼ mile into the wood at the gate, turn left at the drive junction and curve round to the A60 road. Turn right and 100 yards later left into Holbeck Woodhouse. At the cross roads continue ahead on the 'footpath only' track passing St Winifred's church on your left before gaining Holbeck. Turn left then right immediately as footpath signed—Creswell Crags 1 mile. The path is well stiled as you keep to the lefthand side of the first two fields, before keeping to the righthand side for the next three. At the brow of the hill descend to a solitary tree and some rocks and bear right into Creswell Crags. Keep to the righthand path passing beneath the caves with the Crags Pond on your left. Walk round the end of the pond to your left, and just before the road turn right along the path with the sewage works on your right and ascend to the Visitor's Centre and car park.

CRESWELL CRAGS—the limestone gorge is the border of Derbyshire and Nottinghamshire, and the nearby Visitor's Centre is a joint project for both councils. The gorge has yielded some of the finest examples of fossils for the study of prehistoric man and man's evolution. The centre has a display of finds of Stone Age man.

CRESWELL CRAGS TO TRUMAN'S LODGE—
4 ½ MILES

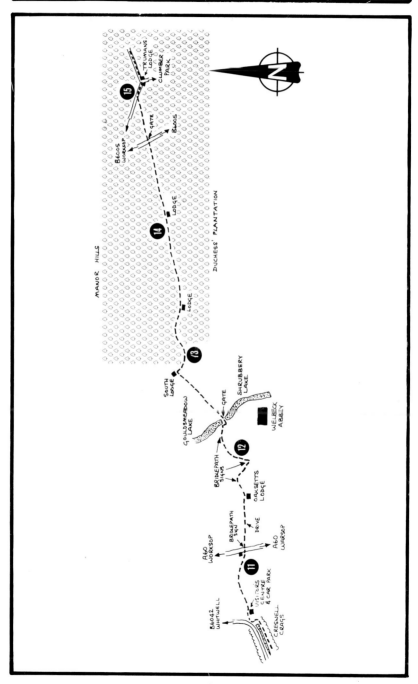

10

CRESWELL CRAGS TO TRUMAN'S LODGE—
4½ MILES

ABOUT THE SECTION—

First you walk around the edge of Welbeck, mostly on driveways to reach Shrubbery Lake. Two fields from here you enter woodland, which, in my opinion, is the finest in the whole area with magnificent beech trees and a sandstone gorge. You keep in woodland all the way to Truman's Lodge.

MAPS—*1:25,000 O.S. Pathfinder Series, Sheet No SK 47/57— Worksop (South) & Staveley. 1:25,000 O.S. Pathfinder Series, Sheet No SK 67/77—Clumber Park and East Markham.*

WALKING INSTRUCTIONS—

Walk past the Visitor's Centre and car park and follow the track through the trees to the A60 road ½ mile away. Cross the road and continue on the Worksop College driveway, signed a bridlepath. Keep on the drive for ½ mile to Oaksetts Lodge, where as bridlepath signed bear left onto a concrete driveway. At the next bridlepath sign cross another driveway and follow the concrete one round to your right to a cattlegrid. Here, again as signed, turn left onto a grass track and follow this for a little over ¼ mile around the edge of the trees on your right to another sign, driveway and gate. Turn right and left shortly afterwards and 60 yards later left again, and pass between Shrubbery and Gouldsmeadow Lake. The pathline keeps to the lefthand edge of the fields as you gently ascend to South Lodge, ½ mile away. Again it is well signed and gated.

At the lodge turn right onto the path, which soon develops to a track after the sandstone gorge. You keep on this path/track for the next two miles to the B6005 road. Ignore all side trails, simply keep ahead all the time and pass two lodges. Cross the road and continue on the track through more forest to a minor road just over ¼ mile away. Turn right to Truman's Lodge, 100 yards away, and an entrance into Clumber Park, National Trust Property.

South Lodge, Welbeck

TRUMAN'S LODGE TO NORMANTON INN–
4 MILES

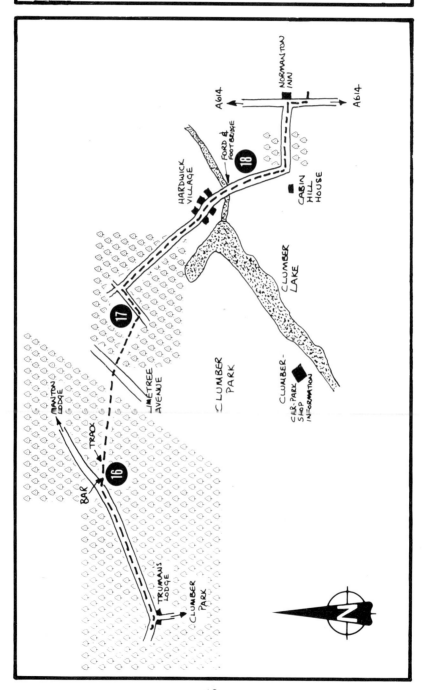

TRUMAN'S LODGE TO NORMANTON INN— 4 MILES

ABOUT THE SECTION—

You pass through further forest in Clumber Park and cross the famous Limetree Avenue. A mile later you reach Hardwick Village on the edge of Clumber Lake. A brief road walk brings you to the A614 road opposite your second inn of the walk—Normanton Inn.

MAP—*1:25,000 O.S. Pathfinder Series—Sheet SK 67/77— Clumber Park and East Markham.*

WALKING INSTRUCTIONS—

Turn left at Truman's Lodge and follow the road between the trees for ¾ mile to the bar and track on your right. Turn right and follow the track through the trees, and where it turns right after ¼ mile keep straight ahead, and after a further ¼ mile reach another bar across the track and enter open country. Continue ahead to Limetree Avenue. On the opposite side and to your left is the cinder path running beside the pine trees on your left. Follow this for ¼ mile to the next tarmaced driveway. Turn left along it, and at the cross roads at the brow of the hill turn right for Hardwick Village ½ mile away. Follow the road through and around the village and over the ford of the River Poulter. There is a footbridge here. Continue up the road to Cabin Hill and turn left, still keeping to the road to the A614 road, opposite the Normanton Inn.

Normanton Inn

NORMANTON INN TO
WHITEWATER BRIDGE—4½ MILES

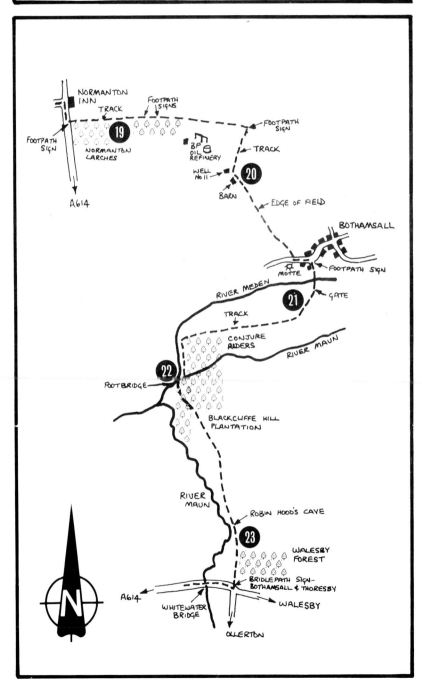

NORMANTON INN

TRACK

FOOTPATH SIGNS

FOOTPATH SIGN

FOOTPATH SIGN

NORMANTON LARCHES

19

BP OIL REFINERY

TRACK

WELL No 11

20

BARN

EDGE OF FIELD

A614

BOTHAMSALL

FOOTPATH SIGN

MOTTE

RIVER MEDEN

GATE

21

TRACK

CONJURE ALDERS

RIVER MAUN

22

FOOTBRIDGE

BLACKCLIFFE HILL PLANTATION

RIVER MAUN

ROBIN HOOD'S CAVE

23

WALESBY FOREST

BRIDLE PATH SIGN— BOTHAMSALL & THORESBY

A614

WHITEWATER BRIDGE

WALESBY

OLLERTON

N

NORMANTON INN TO WHITEWATER BRIDGE—4 ½ MILES

ABOUT THE SECTION—

A mile of woodland returns you to open fields as you head southwards to Bothamsall. Here after crossing the River Meden you head westwards into more woodland to Conjure Alders and the junction of the Rivers Maun and Meden—a particularly attractive place. You continue southwards in further woodland, passing the sandstone outcrop containing Robin Hoods Cave before gaining Whitewater Lane and bridge.

MAP—*1:25,000 O.S. Pathfinder Series—Sheet No SK 67/77— Clumber Park and East Markham.*

WALKING INSTRUCTIONS—

Turn right opposite the Normanton Inn, along the A614 road for 100 yards to the footpath sign on your left. The path/track is well defined and signed as you follow it for the next mile. After ¾ mile you leave the forest behind and see a small oil refinery on your right with noddy pumps. Pass one on your left and shortly afterwards turn right onto a track, as footpath signed. A little over ¼ mile along here at a barn with Well No 11 on your right, turn left and keep the field boundary on your right. This path is little used, but continue ahead for a couple of fields before leaving the hedge on your right and crossing the field ahead to the left of a mound with trees on top—a motte and bailey castle. Here reach the road and turn left into the edge of Bothamsall village.

Opposite The Smithy turn right, as path signed, and pass Meadoway on the track and cross the River Meden. Follow the track round to your right before it keeps straight ahead almost westwards to the forest. After ½ mile the trees are on your immediate left, and on meeting the River Meden again the track turns sharp left to the footbridge over the River Maun ¼ mile away. Cross the bridge and turn right and left opposite the next footbridge, and follow the path through the trees to a track. Keep ahead and ascend the track to the junction. Continue ahead on the track along the lefthand edge of the plantation to a path sign. Here keep right on a path with open country on your left and the river Maun getting closer on your right. The path becomes a track and passes Robin Hood's Cave on your right after ½ mile. A further ¼ mile along the edge of Walesby Forest brings you to Whitewater Lane and the bridlepath sign— Bothamsall and Thoresby. Turn right to Whitewater Bridge, 100 yards away.

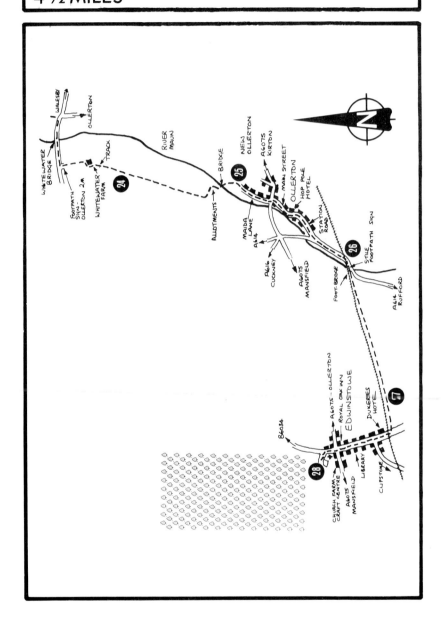

OLLERTON—although close to major roads and coal mines, the orginal village is totally unspoilt and one of the gems of the walk.

WHITEWATER BRIDGE TO EDWINSTOWE—
4 ½ MILES

ABOUT THE SECTION—

The final section, now you can get out the map you started out on! First it is along a track to Ollerton and its charming unspoilt village. The final couple of miles follow a path beside the fields to Edwinstowe, leaving you to walk through the village, replenish your energy with all amenities to hand, and explore the parish church and its connections with Robin Hood and Maid Marion.

MAPS—*1:25,000 O.S. Pathfinder Series—Sheet No SK 67/77— Clumber Park and East Markham. 1:25,000 O.S. Pathfinder Series— Sheet No 66/76—Ollerton.*

WALKING INSTRUCTIONS—

Cross Whitewater Bridge and nearly ¼ mile later turn left onto the track, signposted Ollerton 2 miles. After ¼ mile walk around the righthand side of Whitewater Farm, on the track, and follow it for over a mile around the allotments and across the River Maun. On approaching the houses keep to the right and continue along the track and sometimes tarmaced road—Maida Lane—to the A6075 road in Ollerton. Cross to your left and follow Main Street into Ollerton Village. Pass the Hop Pole Hotel, church dedicated to St. Giles and White Hart Inn, all on your left, and bear right along Station Road. Follow this to the A614 road.

Turn left along the A614 road past the old station on the left, and on the other side of the railway bridge turn right over the stile by the footpath sign. After a short distance cross the footbridge over Rainworth Water and continue ahead along the righthand edge of the fields for the next mile, passing Thoresby Colliery Signal Box. Keep to the right of the houses and reach the B6034 road—Rufford Road. Turn right and pass under the railway and past The Dukeries Hotel on your right, and keep straight ahead through the centre of Edwinstowe to the Royal Oak Inn. Cross the A6075 road and continue ahead past the church, and a little further on turn left into the car park where you began in the morning.

BOTHAMSALL—The attractive village has won the Best Kept Village competition for a population under 300. The nearby 'castle hill' is a former motte and bailey castle. At Conjure Alders the rivers Maun and Meden run as one and are both crossed by footbridges. The route to them dates from Saxon times and the river was forded at a ford named Coningswath.

AMENITIES GUIDE

PLACE	TELEPHONE	TOILETS	CAR PARK	POST OFFICE	SHOP	RESTAURANT	INN	CAMPING	HOTEL	B & B
EDWINSTOWE	*	*	*	*	*	*	*	*	*	*
CUCKNEY	*			*	*		*			
HOLBECK					*					
CRESWELL CRAGS		*	*		*					
HARDWICK VILLAGE			*	*						
NORMANTON							*			
BOTHAMSALL	*									
OLLERTON	*			*	*	*	*		*	*

Greendale Oak Inn, Cuckney

AMENITIES GUIDE

INNS—on the route

Cuckney—	The Greendale Oak, Tel. Mansfield 842377
Clumber—	Normanton Inn, Tel. Worksop 475769
Ollerton—	The Hop Pole Hotel, Tel. Mansfield 822573
	The White Hart Inn, Tel. Mansfield 822410
Edwinstowe—	The Dukeries Hotel, Tel. Mansfield 823584
	The Royal Oak Inn, Tel. Mansfield 822222

HOTELS/BED AND BREAKFAST

Ollerton—	The Hop Pole Hotel, Tel. Mansfield 822573
	Ollerton House Hotel, Tel. Mansfield 861017
Edwinstowe—	Forest Lodge Hotel and Restaurant,
	Tel. Mansfield 822970
	The Dukeries Hotel, Tel. Mansfield 823584
	Friars Lodge Guest House, Tel. Mansfield 823405
	Mrs A Browne, Tel. Mansfield 823211
Cuckney—	Norton Grange, Tel. Mansfield 842666

Hop Pole Hotel, Ollerton

LITTLE JOHN CHALLENGE—LOG

DATE ....TIME STARTED ....TIME COMPLETED ....

ROUTE POINT	MILE NO	TIME		COMMENTS
		ARR	DEP	
EDWINSTOWE	0			
BUDBY SOUTH FOREST	1½			
BROOMHILL LANE	3			
CHURCH WARSOP	4			
CUCKNEY HILL	5			
CUCKNEY	6½			
WELBECK—DEER PARK	8			
HOLBECK WOODHOUSE	9			
HOLBECK	9½			
CRESWELL CRAGS	10½			
A60	11			
WELBECK—LAKES	12¼			
—SOUTH LODGE	12¾			
B6005	14¾			
TRUMAN'S LODGE	15			
LIME TREE AVE—CLUMBER	16½			
HARDWICK VILLAGE	18			
NORMANTON INN	18½			
OIL WELL 11	20			
BOTHAMSALL	20¾			
CONJURE ALDERS	22			
ROBIN HOOD'S CAVE	23			
WHITEWATER BRIDGE	23½			
OLLERTON VILLAGE	25½			
OLLERTON STATION	26			
EDWINSTOWE	28			

BIRD, FLOWER AND TREE CHECKLIST

This is a random checklist of some of the more common varieties to be seen on the walk, depending on the season.

BIRDS

Pheasant
Wood Pigeon
Tawny Owl
Great Spotted Woodpecker
Magpie
Jay
Blue Tit
Wren
Song Thrush
Treecreeper
Great Heron
Moorhen
Coot
Mallard
Cuckoo
Swallow
Rook
Jackdaw
Great Tit
Marsh Tit
Dipper
Blackbird
Robin
Pied Wagtail
Greenfinch
Yellowhammer
Tree Sparrow

FLOWERS

Bluebells
Wood Anemone
Common Vetch
Common Violet
Primrose
Cowslip
Red Campion
Marsh Marigold
Herb Robert
Yellow Archangel
Bugle
Wood Forget-Me-Not
Wood Avens
Foxglove
Lesser Celandine
Stitchwort
Cow Parsley
Ramsons
Dog Rose
Ox-Eye Daisy
Rosebay Willow Herb
Honeysuckle
Great Bellbine
Lady's-Smock
Meadowsweet
White Water-Lily

Deer in Welbeck Park

TREES

Broadleaved—	Conifers—
Pedunculate Oak	Western Hemlock
Sessile Oak	Western Red Cedar
Beech	Scots Pine
Ash	Corsican Pine
English Elm	Lodgepole Pine
Sycamore	Cedar of Lebanon
Alder	Douglas Fir
Lime	Lawson Cypress
Birch	European Larch
Wild Cherry	Norway Spruce
Sweet Chesnut	Yew
Horse Chestnut	
Rowan	

Robin Hoods Cave

EQUIPMENT NOTES—some personal thoughts

BOOTS—preferably with a leather upper, of medium weight, with a vibram sole. I always add a foam cushioned insole to help cushion the base of my feet.

SOCKS—I generally wear two thick pairs as this helps to minimise blisters. The inner pair of loop stitch variety and approximately 80% wool. The outer a thick rib pair of approximately 80% wool.

WATERPROOFS—for general walking I wear a T shirt or shirt with a cotton wind jacket on top. You generate heat as you walk and I prefer to layer my clothes to avoid getting too hot. Depending on the season will dictate how many layers you wear. In soft rain I just use my wind jacket for I know it quickly dries out. In heavy downpours I slip on a neoprene lined cagoule, and although hot and clammy it does keep me reasonably dry. Only in extreme conditions will I don overtrousers, much preferring to get wet and feel comfortable.

FOOD—as I walk I carry bars of chocolate, for they provide instant energy and are light to carry. In winter a flask of hot coffee is welcome. I never carry water and find no hardship from doing so, but this is a personal matter.From experience I find the more I drink the more I want. You should always carry some extra food such as Kendal Mint Cake for emergencies.

RUCKSACK—for day walking I use a climbing rucksac of about 40 litre capacity and although excess space it does mean that the sac is well padded and with a shoulder strap. Inside apart from the basics for the day I carry gloves, balaclava, spare pullover and a pair of socks.

MAP & COMPASS—when I am walking I always have the relevant map—usually 1:25,000 scale—open in my hand. This enables me to constantly check that I am walking the right way. In case of bad weather I carry a Silva type compass, which once mastered gives you complete confidence in thick cloud or mist.

Oil Pump

REMEMBER AND OBSERVE
THE COUNTRY CODE

ENJOY THE COUNTRYSIDE AND RESPECT ITS LIFE AND WORK.

GUARD AGAINST ALL RISK OF FIRE.

FASTEN ALL GATES.

KEEP YOUR DOGS UNDER CLOSE CONTROL.

KEEP TO PUBLIC PATHS ACROSS FARMLAND.

USE GATES AND STILES TO CROSS FENCES, HEDGES AND WALLS.

LEAVE LIVESTOCK, CROPS AND MACHINERY ALONE.

TAKE YOUR LITTER HOME—PACK IT IN, PACK IT OUT.

HELP TO KEEP ALL WATER CLEAN.

PROTECT WILDLIFE, PLANTS AND TREES.

TAKE SPECIAL CARE ON COUNTRY ROADS.

MAKE NO UNNECESSARY NOISE.

Hardwick—Ford and footbridge

OTHER BOOKS BY JOHN N. MERRILL PUBLISHED BY JNM PUBLICATIONS

DAY WALK GUIDES —

SHORT CIRCULAR WALKS IN THE PEAK DISTRICT
LONG CIRCULAR WALKS IN THE PEAK DISTRICT
CIRCULAR WALKS IN WESTERN PEAKLAND
SHORT CIRCULAR WALKS IN THE STAFFORDSHIRE MOORLANDS
PEAK DISTRICT TOWN WALKS
SHORT CIRCULAR WALKS AROUND MATLOCK
SHORT CIRCULAR WALKS IN THE DUKERIES
SHORT CIRCULAR WALKS IN SOUTH YORKSHIRE
SHORT CIRCULAR WALKS AROUND DERBY
SHORT CIRCULAR WALKS AROUND BUXTON
SHORT CIRCULAR WALKS AROUND NOTTINGHAMSHIRE
SHORT CIRCULAR WALKS ON THE NORTHERN MOORS
40 SHORT CIRCULAR PEAK DISTRICT WALKS
SHORT CIRCULAR WALKS IN THE HOPE VALLEY

INSTRUCTION & RECORD —

HIKE TO BE FIT....STROLLING WITH JOHN
THE JOHN MERRILL WALK RECORD BOOK

CANAL WALK GUIDES —

VOL ONE — DERBYSHIRE AND NOTTINGHAMSHIRE
VOL TWO — CHESHIRE AND STAFFORDSHIRE
VOL THREE — STAFFORDSHIRE
VOL FOUR — THE CHESHIRE RING

DAY CHALLENGE WALKS —

JOHN MERRILL'S PEAK DISTRICT CHALLENGE WALK
JOHN MERRILL'S YORKSHIRE DALES CHALLENGE WALK
JOHN MERRILL'S NORTH YORKSHIRE MOORS CHALLENGE WALK
PEAK DISTRICT END TO END WALKS
THE LITTLE JOHN CHALLENGE WALK
JOHN MERRILL'S LAKELAND CHALLENGE WALK
JOHN MERRILL'S STAFFORDSHIRE MOORLAND CHALLENGE WALK
JOHN MERRILL'S DARK PEAK CHALLENGE WALK

MULTIPLE DAY WALKS —

THE RIVERS' WAY
PEAK DISTRICT HIGH LEVEL ROUTE
PEAK DISTRICT MARATHONS
THE LIMEY WAY
THE PEAKLAND WAY

COAST WALKS —

ISLE OF WIGHT COAST WALK
PEMBROKESHIRE COAST PATH
THE CLEVELAND WAY

HISTORICAL GUIDES —

DERBYSHIRE INNS
HALLS AND CASTLES OF THE PEAK DISTRICT & DERBYSHIRE
TOURING THE PEAK DISTRICT AND DERBYSHIRE BY CAR
DERBYSHIRE FOLKLORE
LOST INDUSTRIES OF DERBYSHIRE
PUNISHMENT IN DERBYSHIRE
CUSTOMS OF THE PEAK DISTRICT AND DERBYSHIRE
WINSTER — A VISITOR'S GUIDE
ARKWRIGHT OF CROMFORD
TALES FROM THE MINES by GEOFFREY CARR

JOHN'S MARATHON WALKS —

TURN RIGHT AT LAND'S END
WITH MUSTARD ON MY BACK
TURN RIGHT AT DEATH VALLEY
EMERALD COAST WALK

COLOUR GUIDES —

THE PEAK DISTRICT.....Something to remember her by.

SKETCH BOOKS — by John Creber

NORTH STAFFORDSHIRE SKETCHBOOK

LITTLE JOHN
CHALLENGE

Badges are brown cloth with figure embroidered in four colours and measure 3' wide x 3 ½' high.

BADGE ORDER FORM

Date completed...

Time..

Name...

Address...

....

Price: £1.75 each including VAT, postage and completion certificate.
From: JNM Publications, Winster, Matlock, Derbyshire, DE4 2DQ

THE JOHN MERRILL WALKING BADGE is available to anyone who walks this route twice or has done another of John Merrill's challenge walks. The badges—only available to those who have walked the routes—are circular, embroidered in four colours on a black background. Price £1.75 each including postage, VAT, and signed certificate.